A BIT OF TICKLE FOR THE MIND

A BIT OF TICKLE FOR THE MIND

Poetry

by

Melinda McIntosh

Mike,
Thanks for always
brightening my day
with a smile, a joke,
and a hello. :) Melinda McIntosh

A BIT OF TICKLE FOR THE MIND

PLUS-2 Poems:
contributed by Pamela Gross and Ashley Carpenter

For

YOU

ME

THEM

and

Everyone Else

TABLE OF CONTENTS

Awaken your mind
with poetry

A Beautiful World

Once upon a time...

there was a beautiful world

where everyone loved everyone

and everyone loved them back.

In this world,
the people were all the same
and the people were all different…
and that was perfectly okay
with everyone.

Then one day…
someone new arrived,
sick with jealousy
and festering hate.

The people
in the beautiful world
soon became infected,

the world became ugly,

and no one
loved anyone.

People being the same
and people being different
was not okay
with anyone.

Until the day…
When Someone
came to love everyone,
people were healed,
and beauty returned.

Now, in this world,
people being the same
and people being different
is perfectly okay

…with S *omeone.*

A Bit of Tickle for the Mind

I start with little bits
And the bits begin to grow
End to end
Hand in hand
The bits begin to flow

I never know which path they'll take
Which twist and turn or loop they'll make
I only know
For Heaven's sake
I have to let them go

Not all of them are useable
Not all of them are grand
Most of them are mutter-clutter
And mutter-stutter sand

I keep the bits of mutter-clutter
And all the bits of mutter-stutter
Hoarded like a treasure trove
Of tangled golden bits I wove
Precious gems
Too good to pitch
Now junk plopped in a drawer

They're bits of just-in-case-I-need-them
And someday I just might
In the middle of a poem
In the middle of the night

But today I'm moving on
With the poem now at hand
Trusting that my bits will wind
Beginning
Middle
End
To something that is useful
A bit of tickle for the mind

The sound I want is rhythmic
The thought I want is pure
Some filler-bits
And in-betweens
Will round it out for sure

No I never know quite where they'll go
Or where they'll find their end
But when it works
It's mutter magic
Like finding an old friend

A
Breath
Away

so close you are
　　　to being me
　　　　　I cannot tell apart

　　　where you begin
　　　　　and I'm complete
　　　　　　　love's echo in my heart

Ah, Poetry!

Upon these pages
you will find
poems written
to tickle your mind
with thoughtful thoughts
and mindful finds
and things remembered
of various kinds
…
a cup o' tea
a memory
a quiet nook
…
Ah, Poetry!

Angel

I have a friend, a special friend
Who watches over me
When I am scared or feel alone
She's there to comfort me.

She shows me how to face the things
That make me scared or sad.
She tells me, "Look for good in things,
Instead of for the bad."

I like to sit alone at night,
Just me there with my friend,
And think about the whole day long,
Beginning until end.

The morning sun, the butterfly,
A night of twinkling stars---
That's what my friend and I look for,
We need not look too far.

Everybody has a friend,
A special friend like mine---
An angel sent from God above
Who's with you all the time.

Be to the

Extreme

Take a moment to wish them well
The ones that got away
For in the end
They never were
And be, they never may

Let go of all the could-have-beens
The tears that dampen dreams
Embrace what is
And what will be
Will be to the extreme

Caterpillars

Caterpillars are…
Well…
A little…kinda…ugly
But…looks aren't everything
It's what's inside that counts, right?
And what's inside a caterpillar
Is sorta…kinda…curious
I mean…how else do you explain it…
She puts herself to bed
Wrapped up tight in a cocoon
Then poof!…Next thing ya know
A wing is popping out
And a butterfly is born

God made caterpillars
kinda beautiful that way

Dwelling

Within the Walls of Memories
In the Land of Long Ago
Unable to move forward
There lives a Lonely Soul

She keeps with her the Treasures
Of Yesteryear, it's true
She'd rather sit with Olden Times
Instead of with the New

I visit her from Time to Time
But I don't stay for long
I'm living in the Here and Now
In the Past I don't belong

Everwhite

What is this thing
that I've heard of called spring

I'm not really sure
that there is such a thing

For all that I see here
is snow on the ground

I'm pretty sure winter
is sticking around

Fanny Wrote a Bunch of Poems

Fanny got her pen and pad
And wrote a bunch of poems
She wrote and wrote and wrote and wrote
Some tell-me's and some show-em's

But if you ask her to recite
From memory she can't
For know-em's isn't what she wrote
And memorize she shan't

feather

drop a feather as you soar

that it may brush across my arm

my face

my mind

and I will know that you

are thinking of me

as I

am thinking of you

*F*lash

a soft breeze
blows across the meadow
rain
gently seasons the air

In the distance
smoke rises from a chimney

a sip of tea too hot
burns the tender lips

faster
harder
a rhythmic beat dances on the leaves
pelting its prey

the sky cracks
suddenly
applauding itself
victory over one

before the hearth sits an open book
warm and cozy

unaware the yearning breath
of fire
yet to come

FREE AS A BIRD

you are not a bird that I can hold onto

clip its wings
salt its tail

no
you are a bird that must be free

to come
to go
to spread its wings
and fly

free
to ride upon the wind
like a kite
or a balloon untethered

free
to reach for the moon
the stars
the limitless sky

for only then…
can I

FRUIT OF MY LABOR

I dig a little hole
and I put a seed inside
then I pile upon some dirt
enough my seed to hide

And then I keep it watered
so my seed will sprout some roots
I see my efforts pay off
when up through the ground come shoots

Then the pretty little blossoms
that adorn my growing vine
offer their sweet nectar
to the bees who come to dine

And pollinate the flowers
so that in the end there'll be
a fruity little pumpkin
from a seed grown by me

Hymn
of the
Butterfly

The butterfly's song is silent

Her music is the air

I'm in her trance

Her butterfly dance

As she wings her silent prayer

I Took a Clue from Monday

I was on a path to nowhere
Until I turned around
And saw myself in a mirror
That turned me upside down

I asked myself a question
I answered me right back
I didn't know the answer
So I bought on off the rack

I wore it like a snow globe
My world was not my own
I'd left it laying somewhere
So I called it on the phone

It took me on a journey
Never looking at the map
I lived inside my pocket
Snoring through my nap

Noisy dreams rewarded
Whether day or whether night
Breathless in the mirror
My world was turned upright

You may not understand me
If I rattle in your brain
But I took a clue from Monday
And it brought me home again

i wonder
if it's the same
for my dog

**sometimes
i just need to be alone with my thoughts**

or just alone
with no thoughts at all
so that fresh thoughts
can come in

**my bathtub is the perfect place for me
to be alone with my thoughts**

my tub
filled with water
warm cozy relaxing
water filled with ideas

some ideas will stick to me

only to be dried away by my towel
before i have a chance
to capture them
like fireflies in a jar

most will go down the drain

on their journey
to somewhere else
destined to be fireflies
in someone else's jar

but a precious few

will soak in
and remain
a part of me
lighting my way

i wonder if it's the same for my dog

when he sits in his metal tub
in the backyard
surrounded by bubbles

in the flickering light

of the fireflies

Ideas Galore,

I

Had

2

More

I had 2 more
While at the sink
I can't remember
Think think think

I had 2 more
They left my brain
I must have washed them
Down the drain

Again last night
I had 2 more
But when I woke
They were no more

Now every time
I have 2 more
They're added to
My lost galore

If Our Paths

Should Cross

Someday

We were not meant to be together

…at least not forever

Our lessons sent separately,

were lessons learned together

We gave and took, each in turn,

unselfishly at times

Then we went, bittersweet,

our separate ways…goodbye

Our paths were only meant to cross,

our journeys intertwine

Merely for a moment,

that's how it was designed

Acquaintance or a stranger,

family, friend, or foe

If our paths should cross someday,

we'll both be there to grow

In His Suit That Did Not Fit

I came upon a man once

He was full of spit and grit

With a pinch of salty humor

And a suit that did not fit

I could see he needed money

He needed food

He needed soap

But in his eyes I could see

That what he needed most was hope

I offered him some money

I offered food

I offered soap

And along with that I offered

Just a little bit of hope

He thanked me for the money

For the food

And for the soap

But in his eyes I could see

He thanked me most for the hope

He touched my life that morning

That man of spit and grit

I gave him hope

He gave me more

In his suit that did not fit

It Started
With a Hiss

I don't know when it started

But it started nonetheless

And it's getting on my nerves

Of this I must confess

I was minding my own business
When it trickled to my ear
A soft annoying hiss
And it sounded very near

Suddenly I noticed
There was hissing everywhere
I heard it over here
Then I heard it over there

I heard hissing in the corners
I heard hissing in the hall
I heard hissing in the bathroom
When I was in the stall

Then where usually I hear
Just a bit of quiet yak
I started hearing hissing
Coming right behind my back

Took my troubles to the pastor
For a little peace and prayer
There's a snake in our midst
Need to get it out of there

But never mind my efforts
The hissing didn't stop
I heard hissing in the stairway
At the bottom and the top

I heard hissing in the kitchen
I heard hissing in the loft
I heard hissing in the choir
Though it was very soft

Where a whisper usually sat
Full of chatter meant to hide
I started hearing hissing
Coming right from my left side

There was hissing in the pulpit
There was hissing in the pews
And 'pon my word and honor
All that hissing made the news

The next thing I knew
When I took a look around
It was coming right at me
That awful hissing sound

Well I turned the other cheek
Bit my tongue a time or two
Tried to ferret out the snake
Brought my troubles straight to You

Lord, I'm not very happy
With the way this turn has took
All that hissing goes against
What it says in The Good Book

Now I'm down on my knees
'Cause I know the only way
To get the hissing out of here
Is to come to You and pray

Just Sayin'

When I say what I say

I have to say

I say it

in the way

I prefer to say it

That said

let me say

when I said what I said

I said it

in the way

that I said

I preferred it

But I hear

when you heard what I said

you heard it

in the way

you preferred to hear it

Just say what you say

if you say that I said

what I hear that you heard

I'd prefer it

Late September

When I think of late September
I think of leaves
Changing quietly

From shades of green
To shades of gold
And red and brown

Leaping boldly from the trees that gave them life
To dance
And to die upon the ground

Rustling
As they hustle along with the breeze
Chilly as it passes through

A gentle telling
That Winter's wish
Will soon be coming true

Let Yourself Bloom

In the shadow of a world
already formed
it's hard to grow

Instead of up and out to bloom
the growth is down
and within

And even when the shadow lifts
you keep your place
that's set

In the light
so rooted
in shadow

Can you not?
will you not?
let yourself bloom?

Like Ribbon & Lace

What will they call her?
They just can't decide
Something important
Something with pride

Something that's humble
And kind and demure
Something that's strong
And loving and pure

It has to have character
It has to have grace
It has to be pretty
Like ribbon and lace

A name is important
Not picked in a day
Or even nine months
Least it's looking that way

They've tried on so many
But they're still at a loss
How many names
Can one couple toss?

Should they be worried?
Are they thinking too much?
They still have some time
Or is that just a crutch?

Their family and friends
Will soon come to meet
Their sweet little baby
And tickle her feet

So if she comes early
What will they say?
That they knew all along
They'd call her Nonamé?

Lofty Day

Oh to have a lofty day
A day to run and laugh and play
To read a book or take a nap
To take my time or wear a cap

A day to sing and think and pray
To eat off of a TV tray
To fly a kite or study math
To climb a tree or take a bath

To change my mind just on a whim
To take a breath or take a swim
Oh to have a lofty day
A day to flitter plum away

Mind Games

Put your mind to it!
You can do it!
Easy as one, two, three!

I tried and tried
And tried and tried
It didn't work for me

I stepped away
Went out to play
Let my mind run free

And then it came
A rushing flame
Burning into me

Circle round
And round and round
Take a tip from me

You will find
What's on your mind
If you'll just let it be

OPEN

BOOK

line by line fell the tree
followed every word
I wasn't sure the ending
in the forest no one heard

every page I printed
fuzzy edges blurred
mystery remembered
after it occurred

leafing through the struggles
captured like a bird
you colored up my heart
open book preferred

The

Age

To

Learn

The age to learn
Is whenever you learn
It's never too soon or too late

You're not too young
You're not too old
Today is the perfect date

Pick up your life
Where your dreams left off
Or pick a new place to start

Begin anew
Begin it now
Take back what's in your heart

If you believe
Then I'll believe
And they'll believe you too

You can learn
Whatever you learn
At whatever age is you

The Patterns

on their Plates

As poets ponder playfully
the patterns on their plates

The pitter patter
and splitter-splatter
of spontaneity spake

Within a world
of wandering words
and wondering ways and why's

They dot their eyes
and poke their i's
and spit for spatter's sake

And when they're through
with thinking through
they throw it all away

The pitter-patter
and splitter-splatter
of sputter that they spake

Those playful poets pondering
the patterns on their plates

The Right Move

My chair moved
to a room without windows
but there
I had more light

And with that light
came laughter
and smiles
that seemed familiar
and right

I sat in my chair
looking around
wondering
Who could it be?

The laughter once heard
The smiles once felt
Then suddenly
I realized
…it's me

The Runaway

She ran
She ran
She ran through the night
the moon her companion
her sliver of light

at her clothes branches grabbed
at her toes the rocks stabbed
but still she ran
she ran through the night

no time for regretting
for loss
or for tears
no time for giving
in to her fears

haste
waste
a moment in time
unwell-spent
no reason
no rhyme

chased by tomorrow
faced with today
waste
hastened
a moment in time

She ran
She ran
She ran through each night
releasing the tears
reliving the fears
fretting
regretting
the years spent forgetting

finally forgiving

forgiving
in time

THE VIRTUES OF MANURE:

use the crappy days to grow

Okay, I know it stinks

but sometimes that's just life

Smiling faces turn to frowns

nothing seems quite right

Take a moment to ponder

how to turn the dark to bright

Crappy days are for growing

the sweet bouquets of life

the You
and Me
of We

after the beginning
comes the middle
and that
before the end

over the top
and under the 'neath
around
and back again

wherever you go
wherever you've been
you are
wherever you be

and I'll be there
to hold your hand
the other half
of We

When Nothing Comes to Mind

What is there to write about?
I haven't got a thought
Nothing is what comes to mind
My efforts are for naught

My mind has hit a boredom spot
It's hit a patch of fear
It's overflowed with over-fill
My inner ear can't hear

For neither rhyme nor reason
Have I found that I can find
And nothing takes me nowhere
It leaves me left behind

If I could think of something
I would write about it now
Even for a silly rhyme
I think I'd take a bow

So what is there to write about
When anything at all
Is much too vague to matter
And leaves you feeling small?

The only thing to write about
When nothing comes to mind
Is that *nothing* comes to mind
When nothing comes to mind

Whispers
of a
Mindful
Heart

What are the whispers of a mindful heart
But poems and sketches and dreams
Thoughts softly etched in pastel verse
And bound by elegant scenes

Floating on clouds of tapestry rhyme
Shifting and changing the lines
Quietly courting the angels' wings
Life breathed into the sky

Reach for the pen, the pencil, the brush
Whisper your canvas to life
Born of a million days yet to be
And the stars that light up the night

White Dress Bride

White Dress Bride
had you no knowing
of tempers that flow across tables

Like milk when it flows
from fairytale slippers
to shatter the hearts of the fables

It matters no reason
this night does not shine
the Dark Horse released from the stables

The mirror reflects
a tale grim and bruised
and one best escaped while you're able

Why Must Vacations Be Fattening?

Vacations should be like birthday cake
where the calories are free
or non-existent

You scoff and shake your head at me
as if to say
that's just a rumor
or a myth
…much like those places that I cannot visit
on said vacations
…places like Atlantis, Utopia, Wonderland
and The North Pole

Perhaps it is in those places
that the calories are free
or non-existent

Except The North Pole
of course
as witnessed by the presence of Santa Claus
chubby, still, in his red suit
riding on his unicorn
in the summer snow
while the reindeer are vacationing
on the sunny beaches
of Florida

PLUS-2 Poems

When Pamela Gross was a little girl, she often sat with her grandmother, listening to stories of her fascinating childhood. As a result, a special bond was formed between the two---not to mention a few cliffhangers. Pam is still waiting for Grandma to reveal how some of the stories turned out. Grandma, Dear *is one of Pam's first attempts at writing and shows her natural talent for poetry*

Grandma,

Dear

by Pamela Gross

I thought I would always know
The sound of your voice
The touch of your hand
The comfort of being wrapped in your arms
---of never being alone

I thought you would always be near
Me wanting to know
The end of your story
Don't leave me hanging, Grandma, Dear
---I need to know

Holding you close
In my heart
---You will always be here

To entertain her son, Ashley Carpenter makes up silly stories. To entertain herself, she writes vampire stories. Ashley also writes down her random thoughts when she wants to free her mind. With her permission, I put one of her passages of thought into poetic form and gave it a title. Smile and Put your Positive Pants On *is the result.*

Smile and Put Your Positive Pants On!

by Ashley Carpenter

Ever feel like giving up?
defeated?
lost all hope?
overwhelming sadness?

Sure,
Everyone feels this way
at different points in their life.
It's how we get through these difficult times
that matters...

Hey,
don't judge her
you don't know what she's going through...

Why don't people get that?
Are people so broken
they don't see
other's pain?

There is always something to smile about
even
in the pit
of your sadness.

Wait…
today I woke up
…and I'm ALIVE.
There,
a smile should light up your face.

Wait…
I have people that care
…about Me!
Another smile.

I felt the warm sun on my face today.
Isn't that the best feeling
EVER?
There,
another smile…

It's about time you got over yourself.
The world is going to keep on turning
…with
or without you.
But it doesn't have to…

Negativity
and misery
I don't need…

So if you feel the need to spread that junk
Get over yourself
and **put your positive pants on**…

Smile
because you can **light up someone's day**.

And that

is the best feeling…

ever.

Thank you for reading

A Bit of Tickle for the Mind

I hope you enjoyed it

Special Thanks

Thank you to the many people who have
encouraged, indulged, inspired,
critiqued, or instructed me along
the way to creating this book

…First and always, God, for the dream and the gift

…My husband Randy
I am so blessed to have you in my life
I love you with all my heart

…My sister Vivian, my Aunt Libby, my niece Julia J.,
and my friends Laurel M., Pam G., Kammy D.,
Tasha & Josh D., Samantha & Crosley W., Traci H.,
Ashley C., Cheryl & Brooklyn R., Barbara B,
Cindy L.-W., and Holly
…just to name a few

…And finally, thank you to YOU, dear reader, for taking
the time to read my poetry.

51521732R00058

Made in the USA
Charleston, SC
23 January 2016